Being Bi-Polar
In a Small Town

Being Bi-Polar In a Small Town

A Green Apple in a Basket of Red Apples

Janet Rasmussen

Copyright © 2010 by Janet Rasmussen.

ISBN:	Hardcover	978-1-4653-3880-8
	Softcover	978-1-4535-7366-2
	Ebook	978-1-4535-7367-9

All rights reserved. No part of this book may be reproduced or transmitted in any form or by any means, electronic or mechanical, including photocopying, recording, or by any information storage and retrieval system, without permission in writing from the copyright owner.

This book was printed in the United States of America.

To order additional copies of this book, contact:
Xlibris Corporation
1-888-795-4274
www.Xlibris.com
Orders@Xlibris.com
86888

CONTENTS

ACKNOWLEDGEMENTS 7
PREFACE 9
INTRODUCTION 11
MY BACKGROUND 15

7/7/09, 11:00 p.m. 21
7/8/09, 11:00 p.m. 23
7/12/09, 3:43 a.m. 26
How To Be A Champion. 28
4:49 a.m. 30
7/12/09, 5:59 a.m. 31
7:11 a.m. 34
7/12/09, 4:23 a.m. 36
7/13/09, 4:31 a.m. 37
7/13/09, 5:22 a.m. 40
7/15/09, 9:44 p.m. 41
7/16/09, 7:27 a.m. (☺) **44**
I Think 47

On July nineteenth 49

Today Is Tuesday, July 21. I guess there *is* more to write. 50

Today is Wednesday, July 23, 2009, 6:45 a.m. 52

July 25, 2009 53

7/29/09 7:02 a.m. 54

August 9, 2009 5:30 p.m. 56

August 15, 2009, 7:00 p.m. 59

August 31, 2009, 5:40 p.m. 60

March 3, 2010, 8:11 p.m. 62

A FEW WORDS FROM FRIENDS AND FAMILY 67

ACKNOWLEDGEMENTS

I thank God

I thank Lauren, David, Piddly, Big Kitten, Blondie, Max, Mom, Dad, G-Ma, G-Pa, All the extended family. You guys know me well.

Cynthia, Miss Sunny, Judy, and all my new friends at home and all the ones I've lost for awhile.

The Church body.

Everybody whoever came in the store and let me talk with you.

The entire town. You're the best.

To Kelly.

My hope is that this little book will bless your life and become like a reference book that you slide in your purse or put in your back pocket.

PREFACE

I have a kitchen sink that overlooks our patio. On the sink is a picture of our daughter, a vase of beautiful orange cotton California poppies, and the Serenity prayer, believed to have been written by theologian Reinhold Niebuhr. It goes like this:

God . . . grant me the Serenity to accept the things I cannot change,

Courage to change the things I can,

And Wisdom, to know the difference.

I've had a year of serenity. I've been clear and free of storms or unpleasant change. My life has been shining bright and remains steady. I'm approaching eleven years of being a bipolar person.

I've had people ask me, what does it feel like to have bipolarism? It feels like your body is always humming. There is a buzz in all your fibers and it is constant, day and night. For the most part, you aren't aware of the humm-buzzing until you are at rest. I also have had ringing in my ears for thirty years, but that is not typically a symptom, just an added side effect of being human.

When you are diagnosed bipolar, you can treat it just like you would any other ailment. You may have symptoms that the best of medication can't fully take away, but that's normal. I have clenching of the teeth, constantly, and am using a night guard to minimize it. I also have muscle tension. From my knees down I have the annoying habit of flexing my muscles.

When I'm trying to relax at certain times of the day or night I have to stop and tell myself to let go, releasing the muscles deliberately.

When I am going about my daily routines I don't notice these symptoms as much. If I wasn't on medication, I couldn't write this book and that would mean my quality of life would be sorely jeopardized. I have hope and a faith system and I trust in love. These give me purpose in life and the capacity for joy. You can have joy too.

INTRODUCTION

Please be prepared to see and hear and, hopefully, be empathetic. You are going to experience what is called a "cycle." In my case, I was trying to solve a problem. I'm having this burning mouth and have been off my medications for about three to four weeks. Why? Because, in my mind, body, and soul, I was taking everyone's advice that I could possibly get.

I've tried to mix common sense, humor, and God, with doctors and love. At times I will be talking to you in story form and at other times it's the voice of advice from my own experience. The part of the cycle I'm describing is manic. Just look at the time I've recorded of night or day. This is the break in the cycle you will see. For me a break in the cycle could end up in elevated mania, confusion, broken thought processes, fatigue, and some depression.

I have been known to be fearful of people or situations that can lead to panic, exhaustion, low self-esteem and, unfortunately, some time away from work. Those outbursts are really asking for help. Inside I am asking for help. I have been known to ask for help. Help means go home, Dear, get some rest, check that you're on your meds correctly, and if not call the Doc.

The cycle? Well, think of it like a hula-hoop.

As you go through your day, it's like going around the hula-hoop with your hand. It's the cycle of your entire day's brain and, ultimately, your body and emotions that get high or low or even (stable). A glitch is a break in the mind and body rhythms.

Glitches can happen because of:

- no meds;
- slow or fast reaction to meds;
- an introduction to new meds and how these will integrate with the old meds.

This is not verified by any doctor. It is from my own experience and it will vary with each person and their own situation. Always seek professional medical advice. Please be empathetic. I just had my first experience of real fear. It was not my fear; it was someone who was afraid of what I might do to them. I was volunteering and was eventually asked to stop. Not because I had done anything odd or scary, but I could see in the person's eyes the potential of my flipping out that really was too scary for him to contemplate. I jumped through some hoops trying to see if I could convince him that I was of no threat, but it just was left hanging, and I told my husband I could let it go and get on with my life.

Empathy is the capacity for participating in another's feelings or ideas. Mental health is still a stigmatism and is scary to those who don't really know you. Let it go.

I work for our family retail business and part-time for the school system as a substitute teacher. I also help in a volleyball training camp for young people. I would love to hear from the rest of you, who also have a mental problem, on how you navigate your job situations.

MY BACKGROUND

I am half French (my father) and half English (my mother), raised in the U.S., California girl all the way. I was born downtown Los Angeles at the French Hospital, now extinct; we sold it to the Chinese, it was their neighborhood anyway. Someone once groaned and giggled when I told them my heritage. I didn't get it back then. All I knew was, chocolate éclairs and huge crème puffs were a good thing. Poker parties on real felt tablecloths with clay chips were a good thing. French picnics (private parties) that didn't have an agenda like fund raising were a good thing.

Those picnics were the breeding ground for prearranged marriages. I used to do silly things so the other families wouldn't want me in their family circle. I think that was the cheeky British side of me coming out. I was born French/English, so different from each other which, I suppose, could explain why I am also bi/polar.

You may think, when you hear the word "bipolar," that it is the current trendy disease; however, it has been known for a long time—as far back as the 1850s, originally observed by French psychiatrists. The condition is sometimes referred to as "manic depression."

A bipolar disorder manifests itself in mood disorders: one or more episodes of abnormally elevated energy levels—called "mania, often followed by depression. Sometimes mania and depression show up at the same time. It isn't something I have a personal control over, it just happens without any action on my part.

> *I really hate this computer; it gives me the jeebies and a pain in my right lower back, in between the neck and shoulder spot. It's the same pain I get when I'm on my bicycle.*

Excuse the French in me. I hear that's where the complaining side of me comes from.

Bipolar isn't all bad. Although it gets me into a lot of trouble with my husband and in-laws, it's become the greatest excuse when I do kooky things.

One year I was in the local parade in our little town and I dressed up as a historic figure and rode in a convertible with my Brunhild breastplate and red umbrella singing, "Welcome to our little town. I've come to meet you greet you," all in falsetto. I thought I was doing my part to keep this town's heritage alive. It was definitely a manic moment.

Now don't ask me where my little town is because, although we need you to come visit once in awhile (you know how it is when outsiders move into your jealously guarded sanctuary), we don't want you to move here. We are cute and authentic all in the same breath. But what we really need is for our young boys to go to the old country (where our forebears came from) and bring back to our town those naive young girls to keep us authentic. Keep the heritage alive.

As you will see, my husband, an authentic "old-country" descendant, failed to lasso a young maiden of his heritage and ended up with a surprise package instead.

How do you get this curser to go down? What a pain! I took (a) computer class, why can't I remember how to do this?

I'm so old I missed the computer age and the math age. Our Catholic school was trying to keep up with the Russians or Japanese: Modern Math. I lost that battle.

I believe a teacher called me "Chatty Cathy" one time and said that if she drew an ear on the board I'd talk to it. Another teacher called my parents into a conference and said that I was mediocre. I asked what that meant and my mom said, "average." So guess what I ended up becoming? A teacher. How did God pull that one off?

I have a lousy memory. I used to take anywhere from fifteen to twenty-one units a semester and play a little volleyball. Well, a lot of volleyball. And I still managed to get my credential. Why was it so hard to remember things? If it could all be visual I'd have been the 4.0 student.

What I've come to realize is that when you put English and French and manic and depressed altogether, oh my, you get smorgasbord. But that has nothing to do with where I now live. That is a clue, but by no means a true invitation to come visit me, unless you want to go to my church. It's a really lovely little church and we are so excited about filling those seats. I've tried just about every church and I keep coming back to this one. It's alive and the pastor is just about my age and everyone is really a sinner, really. They've just surrendered to a Higher Authority. A King of sorts, benevolent, protective, gentlemanly like. He never lies, cheats, steals, gossips, or procrastinates, unless there is a good reason for it. I mean the procrastination part.

So I guess I had an idea that I was different when I was in college. Speaking of college did I tell you that I'm writing this book because I only need, I figure, $180,000 to send our daughter to college. She's worth it. I promise. Our friend said he had a $180 and two daughters if I wanted that. I said, all I really want is for you guys to hurry up and come for a visit so I can get out of this little town once in awhile and meet you half way anywhere.

It helps to have been blessed with a sense of humor and a no-grudge feeling. Once I insult you, or vice versa, I forget about it. A teacher friend of mine told me that I live in the moment. My physical therapist said I was noncompliant.

I had a ligament replacement surgery ten years ago, you know one of those cadaver donor ones. I'm sure I paid an arm and a leg for it. What I really hope is that it was someone exotic, not just Caucasian. Maybe that's how I got bipolar? (: My doctor says that I could have had the anesthesia they call the "killer k," and that could have brought on the psyco . . .

I can't even say the whole word.

7/7/09, 11:00 P.M.

I started this account on this date because I've been off my meds and can't sleep.

It's two hours past my bedtime and I'm still awake.

I've got a minute, but not much brainpower left. This bipolar person needs sleep. It's so important to get proper sleep because the brain is usually in hyper drive all day. No caffeine needed. I try to describe it like a dynamo. I knew I was right on, even before I looked it up in the dictionary. Listen to this: *Direct-Current Dynamo*: Field Coils, Field Magnets, Armature Driving Pulley, Handle to Rocker.

Well, anyway, when I'm on the edge I can tell because I feel like my brain is being slowly wound up by a handle, and it gets faster and faster. All day long it can function fully revved up. Vroom Room Rooom Roooommmmmmm until it is all used up, and then the headache happens, and who knows what the night will be like? Crash and burn or maybe total sleeplessness, even though the body is exhausted.

So my advice is, take the pill, go to sleep. You need it. A false sense of creativity is not something to cultivate. It just eats up more energy that you really don't have.

My diagnosis came about ten years ago, right after that surgery. But the signs were there before then. I just didn't know what was happening.

I'm taking the pill (prescription), now; its time to sleep. Good night. See you soon

7/8/09, 11:00 P.M.

Another night of little or no sleep.

It was actually 11:83 p.m. I've got a second or two before my husband sees what I'm doing. This book is on the low and down. Oh, boy, I'm dyslexic too . . . not really. It's 11:38 p.m., and I meant to say "down and low."

So what's the point here? Oh, taking one pill to help you sleep isn't always effective. You might have to take the second one, just like it says on the bottle. What goes through your mind, or anyway my mind, is . . . What if I have to take these things for the rest of my life? They are chemicals!

That leads me to another funny story. Last Christmas I was really in a bad way. I'm sure it cost me a couple of thousand dollars to get through that adventure. I was doing my thing behind the counter of our store and, sometime just before Thanksgiving, I began to notice a change in clientele. Or at least I felt the people were getting scary. Let me clarify.

We have the locals, we have the visitors and their darling relatives and we have those with the way-too-cute dogs.

And then . . . there are the large groups of those who don't want you to know they are together even though you can plainly hear them conversing on cell phones. And those are the scary ones because they take up all your time or divide your employees throughout the store and don't seem to leave with anything fun. We have a plethora of really cool fun stuff that appeals to all ages, sexes, races, ethnicities, religious persuasions, and political preferences. It's the most fun store to have, and work in, in the world. We even do free gift-wrapping.

> *I've been here nearly twenty years. Was it me? Was it another cycle experience? Yes, this beast does have cycles. I once slept more than I was awake for four months and I was taking all the pills they told me to.*

I guess I forgot the funny part. Anyhow, back to my story.

In the store, just before Thanksgiving. I called 911 to the rescue when I saw all these weird people in the store, and my husband called his gal (the psychiatrist) to counter me. I'm not sure who sounded the saner, but I got two weeks off work just in time to finish Christmas shopping, rearrange all the photo albums, and begin translating the French storybook that I later found out was so old that not one person

I knew could confirm that I was doing it correctly, even my father and my favorite French doctor, who, by the way was an immense help in the beginning. He made sure I still had waves that were still working by giving me an EKG.

> *It's time to eat, the acid in my stomach is winning. Be back in a flash. I promise my computer skills and spelling will improve.*

My child says I have to write one-hundred pages to make a decent book. My intention is to make this short and sweet. Something you can carry in your purse or pocket when you need a little shot in the arm and a good giggle.

7/12/09, 3:43 A.M.

The brain won't turn off.

I need the psychiatrist. Okay, I spelt the whole name out this time. No one wants to use the word or hear you use the word. Say "cancer." It's possibly curable. Say "diabetes." We're sympathetic but not turning our eyes away from you. But when it comes to our mental health, that is a difficult situation—not for us in that category. I've been doing this for ten years now, and yesterday I only spent $90 on plastic flowers, two mugs, and a year's membership to the botanical gardens.

What's giving me trouble is this kitten in my lap kissing me and wanting to write its own story. Too cute.

The point is, take all the good moments that you are given and savor them and, of course, share them with whoever can stand to be around you.

I'm writing with one finger and the cat has fallen asleep on my right arm, purring, eyes closed, content smile on face, claws in and out. I don't want to let go.

It's the same with the good days. I found something I wrote for my daughter.

HOW TO BE A CHAMPION.

You are the coach's arm or mind on the court; how do you get your team to win? (Practice, practice). First you have to be able to try everything that you ask them to do. You don't have to be the smartest, you just have to know all the plays, body positions, like when you shoot, pass, jump, like the footwork, and hand flick on a jump shot. If you know it you can first correct your team, then praise them. It's like being a teacher/player all in one. Expect perfection, correct and praise, then tell them to think ahead so the mistake doesn't happen the next time. Anticipate or see what's going to happen before it happens. Use sign language and verbal commands with your team, make up your own so the other team doesn't catch on . . . if you need to! After awhile you'll only need to use head nods and eye contact to talk to your team.

Tell them to shake it off after they have made a mistake and refocus, get back in the game, BE HUMBLE. Be humble.

Of course this can all apply to us personally, day in and day out. Go to your meds guy. In the beginning I had to try several different psychiatrists to get a good one for me, but I stuck it out with one guy. It helped that I really liked him and respected his style and demeanor and he was short and soft-spoken and I asked him how soon would I be going to the big white house with the wraparound robe that they don't let you out of (I don't know that to be true, but you do think about it), and he gently shook his head no, which meant I didn't have a worse condition yet. (: The other team members are your family and friends. Treat them like gold. They are your lifeline and sounding board. Trust that what they are telling you is truthful and in your best interest.

> When I write, stick in the word "God" wherever it best applies. A good book nowadays sells if you use "God" a lot; or is it that a good book nowadays doesn't sell if it has God in it?

See I told you, *cest' la vie*, being bipolar is not so bad. I'm going to stick with God. Reality and purpose and day-to-day living are all doable. By the way, I was off the meds for about a month and it was really fun until the crash. I was trying to solve a burning sensation in my mouth and wanted to know if it was the meds. Just be careful not to drive your family to the edge. They are your advocates. Don't ask your coworkers to monitor you because they like you better when you're a little crazy; you're more fun then. My girl just hates to see me when I'm afraid.

4:49 A.M.

Got to go, I didn't take my Temazapam last night just to see if I could sleep with only the antipsychotic and antidepressant. Temazapam is a good thing. You get that really good sleep. I have three different pills and they are all a goooooood thing. Don't be concerned about your brain or liver or whatever; the docs are trying to do their best. Just stick with one guy or lady and be consistent with your appointments. They treat you better and even give you lollipops and a balloon and a smile if you give them your co-pay that day. *Bon nui, mon amis,* 5:14 a.m.

7/12/09, 5:59 A.M.

The brain won't let me sleep.

My husband is okay. The three cats are fed and the dog doesn't care about eating at the moment. He just wants his morning stretch, a quick race around the yard, because he is one of those mixer breeds that needs to survey the property and then take his command post on the couch to watch the perimeter. Did I tell you I am fifty-six? Some days—most days in reality—I do okay. Today I feel like Judy Bloomberg, you know her writing, kids stuff. Puppy Longstockings from Scandahuvia. She is freckled and super strong and lives alone with her animals in a big house with all the money she needs; I'm soooooorry. Please read the book, it's so good .

I can't find the kittens; yes, two of them. I asked the older cat to teach them about gopher hunting and I think she took me up on it.

The other day the dog wanted out at 5:00 a.m., or was that me? Anyway, I let the dog out and he barked so I was alerted. I looked out the window and saw a smaller dog very close to him, of course my dog wants to chase it off the yard and the two of them go running by the fruit trees. I hear a yelp and it's my dog being nipped in the butt. He runs ahead, and, lo and behold! There's another dog (coyote) at the edge of the lawn. I yell for my husband and we both scream for the dog, he returns and my husband says . . . I can't remember what, but, it was cute. My husband is a keeper.

I had another life before bipolar, it was fun and free and . . . fun and free. Sorry, I'm whining again.

> *The tabby kitten has returned and now is playing with my robestrings. This one is a male. I hope you haven't heard this story before. He's perched on my shoulder, nowdownmyarm aaaah. His little behind smells like pooooo.*

You know what? I hope this book will sell; I have so much I need to do besides send my daughter to college. Fifty-six is a great age to write a book. It helps to have a quiet house, three cats, a dog who eats cat food, and a niece who is going to become a vet, even though she's studying nursing. She'll get tired of monitoring people and get back to those animals; I just know it.

> *The female kitten just passed by—outside the sliding window. All is well in Snooville. The other kitten has arrived, you know the one that needs to type and dniff and cheq and rub222q1q1b oh boy.*

Where was I? This writing is so amateur. Patience, patience, please. I'll get better. Really really. (: Patience is a virtue. What are those seven virtues? I know there is self-control and love and maybe faith, kindness, and self-control? That's seven right? I'm telling you if you come to my church they have made a beautiful wall hanging of them. But watch out for the lady who dances in the foyer she is so into it. I love her. I want to sing in the choir but that means getting up at seven to be there by eight and then I would miss out on the study group before service . . .

> *Love love love the female cat is back in my lap for a second round of love love love , , , ,*

and it might be my turn to be a greeter or a prayer partner and I might have to ditch out of service early to make it to work so . . . Can't tell it all today. I need to rest.

7:11 A.M.

Ouch my right neck shoulder thingamabob is there again. I don't know if I can spend my hundred bucks for the massage. I did hear that in the next town they're going for forty but that's thirty-five minutes away you know . . . gas prices. Is that my mom or dad or I talking? I love bp it is the greatest excuse. I fixed another typo. Yeah! I know what's going to happen to this book . . . it's not going to be one of those classics, it's going to be a period piece only and gets sent to the no-hard-cover section of the library and then to the church 25-cent book by-buy sale table. Hopefully not as one of those "we need to burn this one" because the kids are too smart and we need to help them learn at our pace.

Where is this coming from? I need more sleep for sure.

Do any of you have time to read a book I sure don't, so I'm going to write this in as few pages as possible. If this book goes anywhere outside of California I want it to go to *Guideposts*. You know that Peale gentleman. No disrespect, sir. I owe you a ton. For two years now I've survived on your daily advice. Oh, no, now I'm thinking too much again.

> *Shoot there goes the rebuilding of the cabin that the quake of 1400 cracked the roof and made the tree grow at lightning speed and push it into the side of the cabin that caused the windows to bulge and the robbers to scare the mice out and my husband to swear that junta virus will get him. I bet I get to him first. U know.*

He is a saint at times, my husband. We used to own a cabin in the woods. It was very primitive, but a tree was leaning against it and after fifteen years it has finally crushed in the side of the cabin and one of the major branches fell through the roof so we had to give up on it and let it go back to nature. It was my serenity spot. Find yourself a serenity spot. Everybody needs one

7/12/09, 4:23 A.M.

Wow I'm slowly figuring out this silly computer a little at a time. It's the same thing with anything. I was trying to teach someone how to use a . . .

> Oh, Max the cat, I just love it when you sit in my lap, let your head dangle off my lap and make me type with one finger. He is so handsome until he really relaxes and then . . . there's that perfume . . . I think I forgot to say good morning sunshine. My mind is drifting.

7/13/09, 4:31 A.M.

If you come to our little town I'll find some way to make your day special and fun. I'm not supposed to, because that might make you come back here more often and then we would really have to build that two-story parking lot, and you know what that means? Bigger! No we can't have that. It would take all the fun out of the "Where are the nisse men (elfin-like figurine)?" and, "How do I get to that famous eatery?"

When your brain is almost used up and everyone can see the redness in your eyes, do one nice thing and you can go home to the safe place we all have created for ourselves. A to-do list is pretty darn handy and even more essential when you've lost your keys and the grocery store manager has to figure out your shopper's code again.

Did I tell you someone told me I wasn't crazy I was just getting old. It's another bp thing. Crazy (and you will hear it) and 56, or 56 and old. It's a win-win situation. Right? I'm going to retire with disability benefits. Right? And the 139 dollars a month that the teachers are going to pay me . . . and the garden shop will give me that locals' discount, I hope . . . There I go being cheeky again. Where are the Rolos when you need them?

When it comes to the end of the day and all your symptoms, or lack of meds, have got the better of you, take a stroll. Take off your shoes and stockings . . . feel the whatever on the soles of your feet. Drink that glass of water. SIT DOWN if you can. AND DON'T FORGET TO EAT SOMETHING. I started out with a little breakfast that was good, had a couple of spoonfuls of cottage cheese and strawberries, which I finished off at dinner. And when my family and my mother and mother-in-law called to check up on me and my husband called for the second time and then came home.

♓ ♒♋♎ ♦□○♏ ♍♒♓♍♑♏■ ♋■♎ ❍♋♓□■■♋♓♦♏ *that means chicken and mayonnaise in wingdings font (; it's the cat again.*

People will be there for you if you let them, and I'm seeing that all my town folks are there to support and protect me even if I don't know it. THANK YOU ALL.

GGGGGGGGGGGGGOT TO GO, GETTING TOO EMOTIONAL and sleep may come again with any luck.

Love ya. I have to hand-write a letter to my friend who's in the same boat as me. Remember just one more thing: You can do it. Nitey-night.

7/13/09, 5:22 A.M.

Bipolar is not a death sentence! You can function.

7/15/09, 9:44 P.M.

If you decide to write "the book" don't be afraid to stare life in the face. Go to the nursing home closest to you and breathe the air, call and spend time with your mother, wherever she is, mentally, physically, or spiritually. Now where is this coming from? Let's tell a story. This morning I stole a mole from my Piddly. That's our dog. I call him that because he had to do that for quite a long time when he arrived at our house from the pound. He was a stray on the streets of the next larger town.

This morning when I asked for the mole, he relinquished. Gave it up without a fuss. I carried it gently to the patio. It had a few bubbles around its nose so I had hope for life. I took it to a quiet place so it could rest in the basket I found and gently scattered a little dirt over its body. Not its head, in case it could still breathe. Now it needed darkness and time to rest in case there was an ounce of life that was not ready to give up. I stroked it and spoke to it gently and immediately went for the antibacterial soap, just in case.

Later my sick child who was going off to college and had never really seen a mole up close, that she could remember (I did freeze one years ago on the shelf next to the old coffee beans), was sitting on the chair in front of the TV. So, I asked if I could show her the mole and she said, "I think . . . no thanks." So I had to tell her the story of the frozen one she had missed. Okay, that perked her up a little and she gave in.

So I tiptoed out to the patio and, GENTLY now, pulled away a little dirt, and now she was somewhat interested. "I see the paw and the nose, is it alive?" she asked.

No I don't think so.

So I uncovered a little more, but this time I took it back to the kitchen (see, giving her time to get used to what she had seen) and lowered it to the wooden cutting board where she could now safely view it but not touch it. I did the right thing and began to run my finger along its back to see if it wanted any comfort.

Well, anyway, it had gone to its maker and now it was safe to really look it over good. We touched, we lifted, and we turned it over looking for a reason for its demise. I suggested that it had been squeezed too hard and got its breath knocked out of it, probably by a dog or owl or even a coyote.

The point if this story is: When you start to lose it don't be surprised. Some people will be gentle and some will poke at you and even call you names. You just gotta love 'em. God gave us plenty of people to protect and nurture us in our times of crises. It's the USA, criminy sakes.

Oh, boy! That's just going to bring more people here to my little town and we will run out of moles. I should run out of steam also. Ta-ta, I'll be at work tomorrow. Come in for a chat.

7/16/09, 7:27 A.M. (☺)

We'll start with a point today. I lied! I woke up at five-ish and fed the cats and dog, checked the plants. I lied again. My husband found me out wandering, just in the yard, in my pjs—only the backyard this time. Then I'm sitting at the computer trying to figure how to use or put the date on and whammo! He tells me, "It's off to bed with you, dear." He's trying to do his job—taking care of me.

I got a fifteen-minute neck and shoulder rub. (It was only five minutes.) I'm trying to train him, but we've been so apart (in the same house) for eighteen years, trying to work and raise our young lady, that we just drifted—even though we work minutes apart from each other and do lunch at home. We didn't have to talk, right?

In reality he let me out of bed at 6:00 a.m. and sighed and rolled over into la-la land. The point is, being a family member can be a tough job. Please know that we love you and need you and don't want this manic to be here either.

The animals teach me everything, just like the pharmacist. You don't need wrong advice (I think he is Swedish), you need TIME, time to figure things out using ALL the resources, like docs and meds and health food stores and dentists and even specialists when the time comes, just in case.

Make a plan, don't lose the plan, focus-focus-focus. That . . . .

32w2w2w2w2w2w2w2w2w2w2w2w2w2w2w2w2 w2w2w2w(it's the cat again)

. . . leads to another funny story: I'm in the store and there is this person and I approach slowly this time because, you see, I've adjusted the time I take the medication to help me have "happy time" for a little longer and we are going to keep the store open until 7:00 p.m., so I can be calm and funny without scaring the customers . . .

,,, *forgive me, my thoughts are drifting again let's change the subject.. HMMMM* .

I think the plants teach me everything. Cultivate around their roots to see if they need a little or no water or, like roses, a good long drink. I also found weeds—well so-called weeds in with the sunflowers I planted by seed— and a very long sharp pointy metal object that must have been in there since 1956, or maybe when the rain gutters were installed.

When you are tired you get drifting thoughts.

The point? Everybody has drifting thoughts, don't freak out. Be like an animal, look, listen, dig, scratch, eat, drink, climb, fall, get up, eat some more and you're ready to start the day, after you wash up and put your make-up on.

A tout allure mon amis.

I'm sorry, the kitten stepped on the keyboard.

There will be times when you feel ruffled and out of sorts. Don't be so hard on yourself.

I THINK . . .

I know the bottom line. The kitten needs me. The older cat needs me. The dog needs me. The man needs me. The girl needs me. The fish need me. The grandparents need me. The parents need me. It's time to surrender. Take that sabbatical. I mean surrender, give it up, and listen to the inner voice. It has your best interest at heart, literally.

Oh, don't forget the work and the volunteer committee and the place of worship. I know you all have one, whether it is private or public. Listen to one voice that sets you straight. You can only put your best foot forward, or give one up for the Gipper so many times when you are running on half a tank. Hopefully, someone will bring you some of our delicious candy and pastries. We miss you, *atout a loure,* see you later, or as my English cousins would say, whenever there's something positive, "brilliant."

The point again is that with the meds everything is much easier, slower. I can clarify and organize less and just be pleasant. There is not so much calculated thinking going on. Oh, no I've been up five hours and this is all I've written. Now, I don't like bipolar. I've got to think positive thoughts. As you can tell I'm up—but I'm not running on all cylinders quite yet. It's not time to take the morning meds yet. Look on the bright side. I'm at home and I'm using less gasoline (pills). It can become expensive.

I'm really out of sorts. Look at the time! Everything in my head has become jibberish. If I can decide what I can possibly do in a day, I may miss becoming overloaded.

If I am not at work today, I'll make sure someone will represent me in a more positive light.

I'm not making sense right now. Sorry it's 1:04 pm. ON TO THE NEXT PAGE!

ON JULY NINETEENTH . . .

I had to go into the hospital. This will be my first experience since my knee surgery.

TODAY IS TUESDAY, JULY 21.
I GUESS THERE *IS* MORE TO WRITE.

It's 10:30 p.m. and I'm inspired to slip out of the comfort and quiet of my "Hotel Suite," my hospital bed. As I look out of the window I see soft, angular light coming through the Venetian blinds. The glow of streetlights and building lights are dappled. A car has just passed by with its red reflective taillights, skipping across another blind spot in the shade. I can feel the majesty of this place and so I am grateful for the experience.

I bet you are thinking I'm telling another story; it's the truth, woven into story form. I just have to reiterate how cool and protected and calm I am. I have voluntarily checked myself into the emergency room of our local hospital, and, by my own choice I'm in the psychiatric ward of this fine hospital. I was in a very distrustful state with my family. I got here with the help of my family but, most importantly, I'm here on my own volition, not even knowing what was sent in my path.

There it is! A stunning surprise package. This place rocks! And that's no joke. The staff are truly exceptional employees. They are devoted, yet nonchalant. Protectors and crusaders, mentors, professionals, with kid gloves on. I have a feeling I'm returning to my old self and will be going home in due time.

My family came to visit and, wow! What an eye-opener it was for them. Now they are telling me "we can do this, we can do that." They get it and I didn't have to do anything but open up my heart (right after I got things off my chest).

> *Bark-bark-bark! Now it's a sweet . . . moo-moo-moo . . . milk and honey for everyone and graham crackers on the side, just for the joy of it.*

So don't be afraid. There are no white jackets or shock therapy. This is the twenty-first century and you are in good hands.

TODAY IS WEDNESDAY, JULY 23, 2009, 6:45 A.M.

    Venetian blinds are a miracle! Especially the one-and-a-half-inch ones. They let you take a peek at the world in one-and-a-half-inch slices. For those people who can take into their lives the big wooden shutters, more power to you! That means you are willing to see more and hopefully trust more. I now know what "The Sun Also Rises" means. I got up just in time to catch the sunrise. That one is life changing. But remember, like my brother Paul always told me, "All things in moderation." He is my big brother. That is all I have learned today.

JULY 25, 2009

I'm not sure if this analogy will work, but think of bipolar like a palm tree I observed while I was in the hospital. There is a palm tree in the garden room and it's looking very healthy, compared to the ficus tree. So, I examined it closer and what I saw was that the new palm frond sends out feeler fronds as it is growing. You will also be sending out feelers. That means your emotions will tell you what to do, when to do it and how to do it.

If you are on meds, stay on them. Meds that are given to you by qualified doctors, not off the street. "Be affirmed," everything has a cycle or a path. TRUST. Bipolar is like a roller coaster sometimes. Not very often, but it can have ups and downs, circles and spins. They call them cycles. AS THE SUN ALSO RISES MAY YOU ALSO CREATE GOOD MEMORIES.

Best Wishes,

Janet Rasmussen

7/29/09 7:02 A.M.

I'm coming to the end of the cycle. I've been on my meds for three weeks, as you can tell by the time and the date. I've been able to rest and sleep much better. I went to bed at 9:45 p.m. and slept through the night. I promise it is only a cycle. It doesn't really happen to this extreme unless for some reason you interrupt the usage of the medications. Come see me in about a month, I'll be refreshed and ready to go.

Thank You

Sincerely, xoxoxo

Hopefully, your friend

P.S. When you are in a manic state you can crank this stuff out at "Light-Year" speed. Being stable is where you want to be. I'm hoping to have been able to help you, both sides of this picture, and just to be a little facetious, I'm hoping to never have to star in the movie because I'd have to get my eyelids done. I'm doing them anyway. Grow old gracefully, but for the Lord's sake go home looking halfway decent.

Thank you again. I hope to see you soon. It would be a pleasure to become your friend.

This time I think I can end this book I really want to keep it short and also be an eye opener to those who will be living with bipolar. I'm concerned for those friends and family members. They have a tough job and it can only be fought with love and patience. I found something on line that might be helpful under "user accounts" so I have customized it to fit this book.

Customize the way God and you look for each other on your adventure.

Have your own list of favorite people, and those you've recently visited, visit again.

Help protect your important values.

Have your own set of documents or keep a journal. Keep your files private and use a password. It's important to have somewhere to vent and it also gives you an overview of your day.

Communicate more often. (: Do your communicating without closing your heart.

Well, God Bless. Good Luck. Don't make a mess of things or you might scare somebody or they might just call you crazy. That hurts. My style is to be sweet and leave them laughing. I know what you could do! Go to your local stores for window-shopping or get out of town once in a while.

AUGUST 9, 2009 5:30 P.M.

Be courageous. *Courage*: noun, person, place or thing. Strength to withstand [stand up against] danger, fear or difficulty. Firmness of mind and will.

Be *brave*: gallant, daring, valiant, bold, heroic, intrepid, fearless, stouthearted. This is for the patient as well as the caregiver.

I have a case manager. She has been provided to me through my insurance coverage at no extra charge. I was also given a case manager in the hospital. My insurance case manager and I are on a first-name basis.

Just so you have some perspective, the case manager has told me that there are two types of bipolar.

Type 1 is a more intense form. In type 1 you cycle more frequently and the manic or depressive states ramp up quicker. The good news is you are over it quicker.

Type 2 is milder. Your highs aren't as high and your lows aren't as low, that was news to me. In general, professional people have told me that this syndrome (for lack of a given word) is found in intellectual people. I don't know that to be true. Maybe. Let's define "intellectual" as belonging to, or performed by, a person with understanding of unusual mental capacity. Now that sounds a lot like the average normal person to me.

I spend a lot of time problem-solving. It gives me a feeling of accomplishment. When I can't verbally put three or four words together; I know there is a GLITCH. In my case I have had approximately five major glitches in ten years. All of these have a fundamental common thread for me. I have fear. I can't seem to differentiate between reality and a lot of information that I'm trying to process.

Let me give you the example of last Christmas season. I truly believed that people were in my store to take things without paying for them. This may have been true or not. But, it was my reaction to this perceived behavior that got me in trouble. I literally stood by the entrance for eight hours straight: no breaks or water or food or rest. My brain and body were exhausted. This caused my family to intervene. It was a good thing they did. I could have spiraled downward quickly. As a matter of fact, I did spiral and the diagnosis was "anxiety." I was not physically or appearance-wise anxious, yet I did try again to figure out what was wrong with me. It cost me a lot of money to chase a ghost.

Please believe your loved ones when they tell you to GO HOME. Know when the battle is too big. Ask for help. People really love you. Believe it!!

All people have a purpose. All people have been dealt a hand of cards (genetics). Just be who you want to be within the parameters of your given life.

If I tell you more about my experience, will my experience become yours? I hope not. Like any other phase of life, just do it with someone. And, if you are alone, REBUKE THAT THOUGHT! You didn't come into this world alone; you won't go out alone; so why do THIS alone? You don't have to. Support groups are out there.

Glenn Close has spearheaded a website called Bringchange2mind.org. Please check it out. I also like depression, bipolar alliance:dballiance.org.

Your Friend,

Janet

AUGUST 15, 2009, 7:00 P.M.

I've come to realize that you and I are not always to blame. I've been trying for ten years to make my family and friends be okay with my mental health. Please don't do this. You will become bitter and defeated. We are human. If you are like me you are an overachiever. Give yourself some slack. You need it. You deserve it. You are not being unreasonable. Take Care.

That was me venting. Venting is good sometimes.

Dr. Frank Crane said,

"The people who fail are those who become discouraged over their mistakes. They lose heart, and when you lose heart the best way to get over it is to quit doing wrong and begin to do right. It does no good to weep and despair. We progress simply by watching our mistakes and correcting them. Walking is merely a succession of falls. If we fall let us fall forward. And get up and try it again."[1]

Happy Walking.

---
[1] Dr. Frank Crane, *Everyday Wisdom* (New York: Wm. H. Wisen Co., , 1927).

AUGUST 31, 2009, 5:40 P.M.

I guess I have more to say. My husband and I just finished taking our only child to college. Empty nesters we are. My husband and I just finished a discussion on how I have really hurt him to the soul and if he wasn't the man he is and I wasn't the woman I am, this marriage wouldn't have a chance to continue. The point! Reality sets in; hopefully, sooner than later. If you choose to be noncompliant, you have essentially chosen to live a life alone. Unless God chooses to take this situation away from you, YOU most likely will be ALONE. When you burn every bridge and exhaust every friend and family member; you most likely will be alone. I didn't realize until it was almost too late just how close I came to losing my family, my job, therefore my independence and, ultimately, my self-esteem. I thank my husband and the Lord for not letting me experience this.

Take CARE.

The optimum word is "empty." Don't go there. This entry is the most difficult to write. When you take a hard look at your life you realize that bipolar and other illnesses are treatable. We are given the opportunity to take partnership in our recovery and prolonged good health when we make sound decisions to seek professional help.

God Bless.

MARCH 3, 2010, 8:11 P.M.

I've been well for seven months. The burning in my mouth has turned out to be anxiety related and I am on a medication called Lorazapam. I have found, with the help of my husband, a chart. What a handy little item this is. He downloaded it from the computer and I use it every day. I record the names of my medications, and then I write a yes in the next box as soon as I take them. The chart also helps me record how I slept, if I exercised, if I ate and I left a comment space for my moods. It looks like a spreadsheet. It has eliminated the worry of DID I TAKE MY MEDS TODAY.

I wish I could have figured out my burning mouth syndrome sooner. I have always had anxiety as an underlying symptom. My friend Tony gave me the catchiest little phrase, "Better Living Through Chemistry." In almost eleven years I've been in the emergency room three times complaining of heart problems, stomach problems, fainting episodes, and incoherence. It happened to be Tony's birthday and we invited his family over for dinner. Well, I just had to go into an anxiety attack and leave the party, but Tony, being the friend he is, brought his whole family along to the hospital just to make sure I was okay. As I am being wheeled out of the emergency room door, I look back and Tony yells to me, "BETTER LIVING THROUGH CHEMISTRY." All I could do was smirk because Tony is a rocket man and he loves chemistry, literally. I think he would recommend the periodic table to just about anyone.

DATE	MEDS	TIME	YES/NO	SLEEP	FOOD	FLUID	EXERCISE	COMMENTS

I think I'm going to get a license plate with that on it.

Life is good right now and I need to get this book out there. So that's what I'm going to do. Thank you again and wish me God speed.

Sincerely,

Janet

One last thing. I asked my psychiatrist if bipolar would shorten my life. He said no, unless I abuse it by using drugs (street drugs) or alcohol. That's a good thing to remember. Self-medication is a no-no.

Take care! One other last thing. If you can, be like my mother. She is one hundred percent English. She encourages me to keep a stiff upper lip; just believe your problems don't exist; keep socially active. For the women, be social butterflies, for the men, increase the size of your man cave and invite more people over.

Mother says there is nothing that a good cup of tea and thirty minutes of *Jeopardy* can't cure. Ta-ta.

A FEW WORDS FROM FRIENDS AND FAMILY

My cousin in England:

[Your manuscript] was like you were writing in parts about me and Mike and my experiences; everything you wrote is so, so true, about keeping on your meds and keeping your appointments and keeping your friends and family close. I was put on meds at sixteen years old and I've only been off them for nearly three years now, so I was on them for twenty-eight years, but they helped a lot.

But reading what you wrote brought home to me that I wasn't the only one going through it and some of the feelings I had weren't abnormal . . . you made me open my eyes more to the illness I went through and, at times, still go through, but this time without my meds. But if I got that way again I would have no problems going back on them and going back to the docs. But without my family I wouldn't be where I am now. Reading your story has helped me to understand I wasn't alone. So thank you so so so much.

x oooo

A friend in my hometown:

As you know, I have read your story and you have asked for my opinion First of all, I commend you for having the courage to write it honestly and without sparing any unpleasant details. I can only imagine how terrifying your life has been at times. It is a sad story but writing it must have been good therapy, for you seem to have come through it very well. I feel that if more people have the opportunity to read your book it will be very helpful for those that are suffering similar afflictions. If that comes to pass, you will have done a tremendous deed. Thank you for letting me read your story and I hope and pray that from now on your life will be healthy and happy.

Two Co-Workers:
Co-worker 1, a sistah friend

My observation of Janet Rasmussen, whom I fondly call Miss Janet, takes me back down memory lane.

I met Miss Janet in April of 2008. I had applied for a job and Miss Janet interviewed me. I found her to be very outgoing, warm, friendly, with a bubbly personality that welcomed me and quickly put me at ease.

You can tell a lot about a person by looking them in the eyes. [When she feels well] Miss Janet's eyes sparkle and dance, which prompted me to advocate for her by reading all the material I could on manic-depression, so if she should need me I could help her through it.

My experience with Miss Janet's illness manifested during the winter of 2008, almost Christmas. The store was packed with customers and Miss Janet stationed herself near the front door so she could check each customer's bags before they could leave the store. Miss Janet stood there for nearly eight hours, without a break. I looked at her eyes and there was a blank expression on her face. Some of these customers had been shopping at the store for twenty-five years and they felt humiliated. Miss Janet didn't realize what she was doing.

During these episodes her personality is unpleasant. She takes on a dark frenetic attitude in which she doesn't know right from wrong. When she feels good her whole world is bright as the shining sun and she is a pleasure to be around. But when it's dark I feel like it's raining on her and a cloud floats above her head. I could almost experience her pain.

At first, I was afraid and I would tiptoe around her so that I wouldn't cause any problems. But Miss Janet would have a sadness about her. When I went home I prayed for her and asked my church to please pray for her and her illness. I know that there is no known cure for mental illness but some meds can help cope with the illness.

Co-Worker 2, longtime friend

I have worked with Miss Janet for over thirteen years. Throughout this time together I have figured out that she used to average two or three episodes a year.

The spells start off wonderful! She is very happy. Then she becomes silly and fun. She plays little jokes on us. She is so full of energy and laughter. I love this part of the mania, but I also know what is to come—the crash.

When this happens she slips into a very serious state. She becomes critical of her loved ones and strangers alike. No one can do anything right in her eyes. Everyone is "crazy" to her. Eventually she becomes paranoid and believes that everyone—especially her loved ones—are going to cause her harm.

I understand her disorder; therefore, I never take anything personal. I love her, so I roll with it.

When Miss Janet is stable she is warm and friendly. She is responsible and can stay on the task.

Mother-in-Law

We've known Janet for twenty-one years since she married our son, and we have a wonderful granddaughter.

As a family we have experienced several of Janet's different moods and personalities and always pray for good days—which now have been very good and we are grateful for this. She now enters into family gatherings and everyone understands her and loves her.

Her dog worships her and is the best medication she has.

We just pray for her continued good health, for our son, our granddaughter and for good memories.

CPSIA information can be obtained at www.ICGtesting.com
Printed in the USA
BVOW011644010212

281865BV00002B/15/P